For Stephanie, who has stories to write —K. M.

To story lovers and tellers, especially Julien,
Clio, Felix, Elia, and Milo —M. S.

Library of Congress Cataloging-in-Publication Data:
Names: Messner, Kate author. | Siegel, Mark, 1967- illustrator.
Title: How to write a story / by Kate Messner ; illustrated by Mark Siegel.
Description: San Francisco : Chronicle Books, 2020.
Identifiers: LCCN 2017060503 | ISBN 9781452156668 (alk. paper)
Subjects: LCSH: Fiction—Authorship—Juvenile literature. |
  Fiction—Technique—Juvenile literature.
Classification: LCC PN3355 .M43 2018 | DDC 808.3—dc23 LC record
available at https://lccn.loc.gov/2017060503

Manufactured in China.

Design by Amelia May Mack.
Typeset in Mr Eaves, Mrs Eaves, and Trend.
The illustrations in this book were rendered in ink and watercolor.

10 9 8 7 6 5 4 3 2 1

Chronicle Books LLC
680 Second Street
San Francisco, California 94107

Chronicle Books—we see things differently. Become part of our
community at www.chroniclekids.com.

HOW TO WRITE A STORY

By Kate Messner
Illustrated by Mark Siegel

chronicle books · san francisco

STEP 1

SEARCH FOR AN IDEA—

a shiny one.

You might write about something you know really well.

Or research a topic you'd like to learn more about.

Don't worry if not all your ideas are shiny. Sometimes you have to collect a lot to figure out what works best.

STEP

ONCE YOU HAVE YOUR IDEA, CHOOSE A SETTING.

Only you can decide when and where your story will take place.

CHOOSE A MAIN CHARACTER.

That's the person who grows and
changes the most as the story unfolds.

You can brainstorm and draw your main character if you want. Try to learn all about them before you start writing.

STEP 4

DREAM UP A PROBLEM FOR YOUR MAIN CHARACTER.

It can be regular, everyday trouble . . .

SEA MONSTER SCARES FISH!

Sea monster's tail cracks the tank!

Make the problem worse and worse . . .

until finally, your character thinks of something to do.

Lasso the sea monster?

The mermaid grabbed a kelp plant and quickly tied it into a lasso. She twirled it over her head and waited for the sea monster to surface. As soon as he popped up, she threw the kelp as hard as she could. The lasso sailed through the air and landed around his skinny neck. The sea monster was captured!

STEP 6

WRITE YOUR STORY WITH SO MUCH DETAIL READERS CAN SEE IT IN THEIR MINDS.

When you finish your first draft, take a break and go do something else. Stories need time to blossom and grow.

STEP 7

READ THROUGH YOUR STORY AND MAKE A LIST OF WAYS TO MAKE IT BETTER.

- What if lassoing the sea monster doesn't work?

- What other animals at the aquarium can help?

  Sardines!   Sharks!
        Octopus!

- Add details about the sea monster's rage: splashes and thrashes, whips his tail.

- So she ... magic ... The sea ar... came to ...

Reading out loud helps, especially if you can read to a friend. Sometimes, friends see things in our stories that we don't.

She couldn't hold on much longer.
Just in time, a school of sardines arrived.
They swam silver circles around the sea
monster to confuse him while an octopus
raced in with more kelp lassos and tied him
up. "Sharks!" the mermaid called.

In a flash, ~~too~~ two great white

~~S~~She ~~lassode~~ lassoed them to catch a

monster's ropes and leaped over the

STEP 8 When you've finished revising and your story is as captivating as it can possibly be,

READ THROUGH A FEW MORE TIMES.

Make sure every sentence starts with a capital letter and ends with punctuation. If you're not sure how to spell a word, now is a good time to check.

harks answered the mermaid's call
ride! Together, they grabbed the sea
edge of the tank—

CHOOSE A CAPTIVATING
TITLE FOR YOUR STORY,

and give it illustrations,
if you want.

Pictures help tell
stories, too.

The Mermaid
and the
Monster

STEP 10

SHARE YOUR STORY
WITH A FRIEND.

Or two.
Or maybe lots of friends.

When your story is over and everyone's gone, start searching for a new idea that wants to be written . . .